Diary of a *Farting* Villager

An **Unofficial** Minecraft Book

By,

M.T. Lott

Table of Contents

Chapter 1

My name is Bartholomew Johnson, and I am a ten-year-old villager. I live in a village near the ocean. It's pretty nice here. I like to play in the water and walk along the beach. I just have to be careful to avoid the drowned zombies lurking just off shore.

I guess I have a fairly normal life for a young villager ... hurrr ... except for one thing. And, I'm going to tell you that thing right now. But, you have to promise not to laugh.

No seriously, **promise**.

Okay.

Here it goes ....

I have uncontrollable fart gas.

Stop laughing!

You promised!

Seriously. Stop!

It's not my fault, so stop laughing. I mean, it's just something I was born with.

I suppose it wouldn't be so bad if I just had uncontrollable gas from time to time, but it's also really stinky.

Like, nasty stinky.

You see, my family harvests kelp from the ocean and mushrooms from a nearby mooshroom island to sell to players and wandering traders. Because of this line of work, my family's diet is mostly dried kelp and mushroom stew, with the occasional fish thrown in.

The problem, as you may have already guessed, is that eating dried kelp and mushroom stew all the time

3

leads to pretty stinky gas for anyone, but especially for me. The doctor calls it "flatulence," which is just some fancy science word for "super loud ripping farts."

Anyway, when I was a little baby, so my mom tells me, it was funny that I farted all the time. It was even funny when I was a toddler because, well, even the average toddler tends to fart a lot.

But, as I got older and started elementary school, it wasn't funny anymore. And, the older I got, the smellier my farts got.

Graph of Fart Humor and Smell vs. Age

Funny | Death

Humor | Stink

Disgust | No smell

0 1 2 3 4 5 6 7 8 9 10

Age

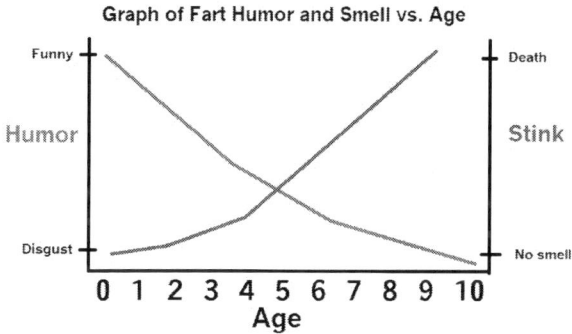

The teachers started making me sit in the back of the room during kindergarten and first grade so that my farts wouldn't disrupt their teaching. Back then, it was just because of the noise, but it got worse as the smell became more and more … hurrr … pronounced.

For a while, they made me sit outside the classroom, leaning my head in the window. But my mom complained that this was unfair treatment and so they built a glass

5

block enclosure for me in the corner of the classroom. A narrow pipe enters the glass box so I can hear what is being said and ask questions. A large pipe goes up through the center of the glass box, to vent my fart gas outside so it doesn't disgust the rest of the kids in class.

When it's time for recess, they can't keep me locked up in the glass box, so I go outside and play. But very few people want to play with me because of my farts.

I've even designed special underwear made of lamb's wool mixed with powdered coal in order to help filter the stench, but it only reduces the smell by about 50 percent so most of the kids still avoid me.

The few kids who will play with me tend to stand upwind of me so that when I do fart most of the odor blows away from them. When they misjudge the direction of the wind, I can see it in their faces. They wrinkle their noses and, if the smell is bad enough, their skin turns green and they have to work hard not to barf.

It really makes me sad.

Despite all of this stinky stuff, I do have a best friend whose name is Stanley Leaf. He's a good guy and actually was one of the people who helped me to develop my special fart filtering underwear. He even made himself a special fart filtering mask out of the same material. He tells me he can barely smell anything when I am wearing my filtering underwear and he wears his mask.

I wish I could understand his speech a little better when he's wearing the mask, but at least he hangs out.

I guess the worst part about it all is being named Bartholomew Johnson. I like the name Bartholomew; it is a strong name.

But, you know what is short for Bartholomew, don't you? Bart. And you know what Bart rhymes with, don't you? Fart.

You can imagine the nicknames. Bart the Fart. Farty Barty. Barty rips Farty. And, my least favorite, BFF, which stands for Bart Farts Forever.

But, enough of feeling sorry for myself. It's time to tell you a story about how my farts actually came in handy for a change.

Chapter 2

It all happened about six months ago, near the end of my fourth grade year at my village elementary school. My teacher, Mrs. Turtle – yes, that was her name, announced to the class that we would be going on a field trip to the Nether.

The Nether?!? I thought. *Awesome!*

I'd heard a rumor that a field trip to the Nether was part of fourth grade, but I didn't really believe that rumor. I didn't have any older siblings who could have verified it for me. I just assumed the rumor was created by the older kids to make fun of us to see how gullible we were. But now, the teacher actually announced it!

"If you want to participate in this field trip, you will need to get permission from your parents. I have a stack of permission parchments here on my desk. Take one on the way out and bring it back tomorrow signed by at least one of your parents," said Mrs. Turtle. "The trip will be next week, so if you don't bring the permission slip back, you can't go."

About ten minutes later class was over for the day and all the kids were streaming up to the teacher's desk to grab a permission slip. I walked up and grabbed my permission slip too, just as I let out a gigantic blast.

FRAAAAP!

"Don't tell me you're going to go to the Nether," sneered Cynthia Brown, wrinkling her nose as the stench of my fart reached her face.

"Yeah, it smells bad enough down there already, without your pollution," said Jane Goodkind, holding her nose.

I grabbed my permission slip and felt slightly ashamed. "I'm sorry. But I want to see the Nether. I'll stand at the back of the class so my farts won't bother you," I said, just as a silent but deadly fart slipped out.

At that moment, someone bumped me from behind. It was a hard bump. A mean bump. I looked over and saw it was Josh Green, the class bully.

"Ouch. Don't bump me," I said, farting in his direction for emphasis. *Ppppffst!*

Josh waved his hand in front of his face, trying to keep the fart smell from getting into his nostrils. By the look on his face, he was unsuccessful. "Get out of here Farty Barty. I don't want you down in the Nether ruining this field trip. I need to show those zombie pigmen just how cool I am."

I laughed at Josh. The unfortunate side effect of laughing is that I tend to let out one fart for every chuckle. So in this case I let out about five or six. *Riiiip. Screeeet. Pfffssstrd. Blurgh. Fraaooop!*

When I stopped laughing and farting, I said, "What do you care what the zombie pigmen think about you? I'm sure their definition of cool is totally different than yours."

I could tell that I had confused him. But he wouldn't admit it. "Whatever Nasty Bart. I wish they could keep you inside of your glass jail while we were down there. Or maybe stuff you inside of a slime."

Cynthia, who had been listening to this exchange, giggled and said, "But that would be cruel to the slime. It would probably inflate with fart gas and then explode."

I turned red with embarrassment and let out another fart, trying to keep it as quiet as possible, but failing.

Sssppuutter.

Josh backed away with a disgusted look on his face and said, "You are so nasty. Don't walk in front of me on the way home."

And with that, Josh, Cynthia, and Jane walked quickly away, leaving me alone holding my permission slip.

As I walked out of the classroom with my head hung low, trailing a stinky fart cloud behind me, Stanley, who had donned his anti-stink mask, approached. "Don't listen to those guys. You can't help it that you have to fart all the time. You were born that way."

I sighed. "I know, people should be able to forgive you for things that you have no control over. They think it's all your fault, even when it isn't. It's not fair."

Stan put a comforting arm on my shoulder and told me to cheer up. "Look, I'm your friend. And that's all that matters. I'm sure someday a doctor will find a way to reduce your flatulence and then you'll be able to hang out with more people. In the meanwhile, maybe you'll be able to develop an even better fart filtering underwear that will filter out all of the stink."

I nodded my agreement, releasing a small fart in the process. *Shizzzing.* It was sad that the only reason I paid attention during science class was to try to figure out a better filter for my farts. But, at least I was learning something.

Stan lived about five houses away from mine, so we usually walked to and from school together. As we walked along the streets, the other villagers avoiding walking closely behind me. Everyone in the village knew my problem, so they no longer pointed and stared, at least not the adults. They were polite enough just to cross the street or wait until I had passed a significant distance before embarking on their own walks.

After about a ten-minute walk, we arrived at my house and Stan asked, "Do you want to play for a while? I have some chicken jockey action figures in my inventory. We could pretend we were raiding a village or attacking some wimpy noob players?"

I laughed and farted. *Sssughughting!* "That sounds like fun, but I want to talk to my parents about this Nether field trip. I have a feeling they're going to put up a bit of a fight."

Stan nodded his head. It looked like he was smiling, but most of his mouth was obscured by his anti-fart mask. "Okay," he said as he backed away from my house and removed his mask. "I'll see you tomorrow morning for the walk to school, right?"

I nodded my head forcefully, expelling another fart – *zzuummbooie* – and said, "You betcha."

Chapter 3

Just as I had suspected, my parents weren't too keen on me going to the Nether, even with adult supervision.

"What if you get lost?" worried my mother.

"What if some zombie pigmen attack you?" asked my father.

"What if you fart on a magma cube?" said my little baby sister, Jennifer, who still thought my farts were funny and not gross. *I wished she would never grow out of this phase....*

I sighed, shook my head, and farted. *Glugeraglug.* "They have chaperones for that. I heard they actually have an agreement with some zombie pigmen to take us on a tour. It's all arranged. There's no danger whatsoever." I said, not really knowing what I was talking about, though it was true I had heard that.

My mother clutched her robe close to her chest, anxiously rubbing her fingers on the fabric. "I don't know. Fourth grade seems a bit young to go to the Nether."

"Well, I don't know about that," said my dad. "I have to admit that I went to the Nether during third grade, but my older brother took me there without my parents' permission."

My mom hit my dad's shoulder and said, "Franklin, why are you saying this in front of Bartholomew? Now, I can't claim he's too young to go."

My dad shrugged. "I just want him to have some fun. These kids are so mean to him because of his condition, and the Nether seems like a good place for someone with stinky fart gas to blend in, if you know what I mean."

"What do you mean, Daddy?" asked my sister.

"I just mean that the Nether smells pretty bad. It is all hot and dank and steamy. And, I'm sorry Bartholomew, but sometimes your farts are quite disturbingly nasty. Down there, in the Nether, maybe the rest of the kids will treat you ... more like ... hurrr ... a normal kid."

And there it was, my parents thought I was a freak. Well, my dad did anyway. I should want to be angry at him, but I wasn't. I guess I kind of was a freak. I mean, I didn't want to be. I couldn't help it or anything, but farting every few seconds is a bit bizarre.

"It's okay, Dad," I said before ripping the loudest fart I'd let go in a week.

PFFRRRAAAAPPPPPPPITITY ....
FRAP!

It even lasted for about five seconds. My baby sister laughed so hard I thought she was going to tip over her highchair. My dad and mom just rolled their eyes and prepared for the smell.

"Maybe I can become an explorer of the Nether and avoid farting in the Overworld so it won't get all polluted."

My dad shook his head. "That's not what I meant. I just meant that … well … hurrr … the kids will be smelling things far worse than your farts while they're down there."

"Like what?" I asked, actually a bit interested.

"Well, the zombie pigmen are undead mobs. And, as you know from our rare encounters with zombies, the undead smell quite horrid. Even a fart created from dried kelp and mushroom stew doesn't smell quite bad as rotting flesh. At least, I don't … hurrr … think it does."

I farted – *brunipth* – and said, "Thanks, Dad, that makes me feel a lot better."

I didn't really mean it, but he was trying. It must've been hard having a son who constantly farted and was never invited to play with the other kids or be on any sports teams. My dad had been a great outdoorsman when he was younger. He'd hiked up all the mountains in the surrounding area and had completed long ocean swims, fighting off the drowned zombies along the way. He was a man's man and I was just a gassy weirdo.

"I still don't think you should go," said my mom.

"Now Linda, we have to let him go," said my dad. "It'll do him good. And besides, he'll be there with his teachers and some other adults and all the other kids. Nothing is going to happen."

I could tell my mom wasn't convinced, and the silent but deadly fart I just released while my dad was talking wasn't helping her concentration, but she finally relented. "Okay. I guess I can sign the permission slip." My mom reached out and grabbed the permission slip and signed the bottom. She passed it over to my dad and he signed.

"I want to sign it too," whined my sister.

I looked at my sister and said, "You don't even know how to write."

"Maybe not, but I can fart," said my sister before squeezing out a tiny little toot. *Zzzeet.*

I laughed. "You call that a fart!" I said before unleashing a blast that was so loud it echoed through the house. *Shsssammammmammaabblooopadurd!*

Chapter 4

The next day, Stan met me in front of my house and we walked to school together. He said he had to spend a few minutes convincing his parents to sign the permission slip too.

"I wish parents weren't so overprotective," I said. "We're ten years old after all."

Stan shrugged. "I guess they think we're still little babies."

At that point Stan's older sister, Gretchen, walked by. Gretchen was sixteen years old and almost twice as tall as each of us. She apparently had overheard what we had been talking about because she stopped and loomed above us before saying, "You guys are just about the size of babies." Then she laughed.

I involuntarily farted as she was laughing. *Quanteeekop.* The stench went up into her nostrils and her laugh quickly turned into a choking noise. She waved her hands in front of her face and said, "Bart, why? Couldn't you hold it in for a few more seconds?"

I turned red with embarrassment. "I'm sorry, Gretchen. You know I can't help it."

Gretchen pinched her nose shut so she couldn't smell the fart gas. Despite her obvious disgust, she managed to smile a kind smile and said, "I'm sorry. I didn't mean to sound harsh. It's just that smelling those farts is nasty."

I nodded my head in acknowledgment, and somewhat in shame. Gretchen trotted off with her other high school friends leaving Stan and me alone to walk to school.

The rest of the walk was uneventful. Stan and I talked about random things. He told me a zombie had been banging on their house last night. That happens sometimes. We villagers were used to it and just tended to sleep through it. But Stan said this zombie was banging particularly roughly on their house. His dad and threatened to go out there and kill it, but his mom had kept him inside, fearing the zombie would get the better of him.

When we finally arrived at school, I put my permission slip on Mrs. Turtle's desk. Josh, the bully, saw me dropping it off. "Great! You *are* going," said Josh with a vicious edge in his voice. He looked over at Stan and asked, "How many emeralds will you charge me for one of those anti-fart masks? I think I'm going to need one."

Cynthia and Jane laughed at Josh's joke.

"They're not for sale," said Stan.

Josh rolled his eyes and said, "Whatever. I could make one myself if I wanted to."

"I doubt that, Josh," I said. "When was the last time you crafted anything? I heard your mom and dad even brush your teeth in the morning." I farted at the end for emphasis. *Durbubood.* I was sick of always being bullied and picked on by Josh.

All the kids in class laughed. It was a common rumor that Josh was completely inept at crafting anything. I thought maybe that's why he was a bully, because of his lack of any practical skills. Maybe he was just as different as I was, in his own way. But he was more lucky than I was ... at least he didn't smell.

Josh briefly turned red with embarrassment at my joke but then got up and punched me in the shoulder before the teacher could could see it.

I rubbed my shoulder and farted on him as he walked away. *Shurpaterpa.* I think he got the better of the exchange. My shoulder really hurt.

At that moment the bell rang to signify the start of the school day. The teacher looked at me and said, "Bart. Get into your glass cube so I can start class."

"Yes ma'am," I said dejectedly, farting one last time – *rapperdapper* – as I walked past Josh and into my prison.

"Okay class, I see that most of you have returned your permission slips. Our trip to the Nether will be in five days, next Tuesday. Be sure to arrive at school early. We will build a Nether portal and then transit to the Nether where we will be led on a tour by a zombie pigman and a blaze."

Everyone had been dutifully writing down this information, but when the teacher let us know that we would actually meet a zombie pigman and a blaze, everyone gasped. I gasped and farted. *UrrrrTABBAtabba.*

"Can we ask them questions about stuff?" asked Stan.

The teacher nodded her head. "I'm sure you can ask them all sorts of questions about ... *stuff.*"

"Are there any zombie pigmen kids or blaze kids?" asked Cynthia. "I'd love to hear what it's like to be a kid in the Nether."

The teacher looked somewhat confused and said, "Well, I know there are baby zombie pigmen. I've never heard of a baby blaze though. But, you can ask your tour guides next week."

The kids peppered Mrs. Turtle with some more questions, most of them fairly ridiculous, and she did her best to answer them all. After about ten minutes however, she was clearly sick of this and wanted to get on with the day's lesson about how to determine how many emeralds you should charge for any given trade.

"Okay kids, that's it. No more questions. Let's start learning how to make as much money as possible."

All the villagers rubbed their hands together greedily, even my friend Stan. I too wanted to learn how to make lots of money, it's the villager way, after all, but I knew that if I kept farting like this, no players would want to ever trade with me. They'd be too busy holding their noses and restraining their gag reflexes.

Sometimes I wondered what the point of all this was anyway.

Chapter 5

It seemed like it took forever for Tuesday to come, but it finally did.

I jumped out of bed, wide awake, and immediately got dressed. I even put on an extra layer of fart filtering underwear, in the hopes that perhaps the smell of the Nether would finally be more smelly than my (filtered) farts. Maybe it was a place I could actually fart without getting dirty looks from everyone around me.

The only problem with wearing two pair of underwear is that it made my robe look all puffy in the back, like

I had an extremely disorganized and overstuffed inventory.

When I walked downstairs, my mom immediately noticed. "Why does your robe look all lumpy in the back?"

"I put on an extra pair of fart filtering underwear," I said, not wanting to hide anything from my mom.

She shook her head. "You don't need to do that. You don't even need to where any fart filtering underwear."

Now, it was my turn to shake my head. "You and I both know that's not true. I can't just unleash the kelp and mushroom farts onto the world directly."

My mom laughed. I farted. *Giggooliddltik.* It was a typical morning at the Johnson household.

My mom handed me a small wooden chest and said, "Put this in your inventory. I filled it with some food and drinks for you to have while you are in the Nether."

I took the box and put it into my inventory. "Thanks, Mom."

My mom smiled. At that moment, I heard my dad walking down the stairs.

"Good morning, Dad," I said.

"Mornin', Daddy," said my little sister, who was sitting in a highchair at the table.

"Good morning, kids," he said. "Are you ready for your adventure, Bart?"

I smiled. "I sure am. Mom just gave me some food and everything."

My dad smiled. "That's great, Son. Why don't you sit down and have some breakfast, and then I'll walk with you to school."

I sat down and ate some kelp and mushroom stew, as usual. As I was finishing my breakfast, my mom brought out an apple pie.

"Have slice of apple pie. This is a special occasion," she said.

I smiled and greedily grabbed a slice of pie and stuffed it in my mouth, barely chewing it before I swallowed it. "That's good pie, Mom. Thanks."

She shook her head at the gluttony I had displayed. "Why don't you have another one, and this time chew."

I laughed and farted – *pooffingitig* – as I grabbed another piece. As I chewed it, slowly, I tasted the delicious fruit and wished that we could eat more food like this, not just kelp and mushroom stew.

After breakfast was over, my dad walked with me to the school. I saw that Stanley's father was walking with him as well. I guess it was a big deal when your kids went to the Nether for the first time. We all formed a group and walked to school together. Our two dads walked in front of us while we walked behind, mainly so they wouldn't have to smell my fart gas.

When we arrived at school, we saw that most of the kids' parents had showed up as well. In fact, the only kid whose parents hadn't showed up was Josh the bully. I started feeling sorry for him again. Maybe he didn't have any parents?

We all stood in a grassy area of the schoolyard. The principal, Mr. Blockhead, pulled a large blanket from a pile revealing a supply of obsidian blocks, which would be needed to build the Nether portal. He and the school custodian, Mr. Oak, quickly put the Nether portal together.

Once the portal was complete, the principal looked at us and said, "Kids, the fourth grade field trip to the Nether is always a ... hurrr ... momentous occasion. For most of you it will be your first time away from home without your parents. I expect you all to behave. We have made arrangements with a zombie pigman and a blaze to give you a tour of the Nether. The tour should last two or three hours, at which time there will be a break for lunch and then there will be a question-and-answer period with Nether mobs, after which you will return home and be dismissed from school at the normal time."

This trip sounded awesome! I farted like five times during his brief speech because I was so excited. *Frap. Blap. Drap. Nrdrap. Googldurp.*

Excitement tends to make me more gassy than normal, and less able to hold them in.

All the kids cheered, excited for what was to come.

Mr. Blockhead produced a flint and steel from his pocket and struck it in front of the Nether portal, activating it. We saw the strange purple and black swirls undulating back and forth inside the rectangular portal.

I suddenly felt nervous. I suddenly felt like this was a passage into the unknown. A passage to doom? Somewhere that I might really not want to go. But I told myself it was just nerves, just anxiety about doing something I had never done.

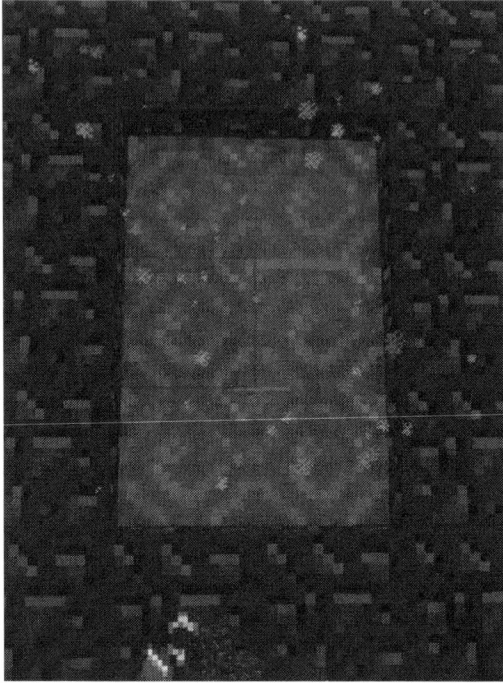

"Okay, kids," said our teacher Mrs. Turtle. "Get in line and hold hands. We're going to the Nether."

Everyone cheered. I knew they'd want me at the end of the line so I stood in the back. My dad shook my hand and said, "I hope you have fun, Son. I can't wait to hear all about it."

I smiled at my dad and farted. *Congrubalubbadubdub.* "Thanks dad. I hope it's fun too."

Stan came over and stood in front of me and then one of the chaperones, vice principal Mrs. Coal, came to the end of the line. When she saw that I was the last student, she stood just in front of Stanley holding his hand, with me in the back.

"Sorry, Bart, normally I stand in the back of the line but ... hurrr ... you understand."

I nodded my head. "No big deal, Mrs. Coal. I'm used to being in the back of the line." It was sad but true. I was used to it. I let out a slow sad fart for emphasis. *Sssspppppiiiittttzzzzz.*

Our teacher stood at the front of the line, holding Cynthia Brown's hand. Cynthia liked to be the first in line and usually was. "Okay, children. Here we go. Don't let go of the hand in front of you."

And with that, we walked like a giant villager snake into the Nether portal.

Chapter 6

I was surprised how quickly we arrived in the Nether. I basically stepped into the portal, there was a weird shimmering wave of light that seem to pass through my body, I farted (*bulpdrupshmoo*), about four seconds passed, and then we were in the Nether. We were all still holding hands.

The first thing I noticed was the smell. It was dank and warm, like a pile of rotting wood. It smelled old and gross, not unlike some of my farts. *Maybe I could fart down here without grossing out anyone?*

"Don't let go of anyone's hand until I count everybody," said Mrs. Turtle. Our teacher walked up and down the line counting everyone twice. When she was assured that everyone had made it through the portal, she said, "Okay, you can let go of each other's hands, but always keep me in sight. If you ever lose sight of me, scream for help."

It seemed a bit dramatic, but I certainly didn't want to get lost in the Nether. I would scream for help and fart too! Someone would find me eventually.

At that moment a zombie pigman and a blaze came around the corner. I reflexively reached in my inventory and pulled out an iron sword.

(I know an iron sword is pretty weak, but as a ten-year-old villager, it was the best that I had.)

I noticed that a few of the other kids and pulled out weapons as well. The zombie pigman and blaze just chuckled.

The blaze said in a guttural voice, "There is no need for that, children. We are your tour guides."

My teacher looked at us and got red in the face. "I can't believe you children. Put your weapons away." We all put our weapons away.

The zombie pigman now spoke. He had a gravelly slow voice. "Children. Welcome to the Nether. My name is Zane Porkchop, and my fiery friend here is Bernard, but we call him Bernie for short."

I laughed at their names. I thought it was funny that a zombie pigman's name had the initials Z.P. and that the blaze's name sounded like the word "burn."

The zombie pigman looked at me and said, "Why are you laughing at our names?"

I farted – *nununblargh* – and then explained that it was odd about the initials and the blaze's name being related to fire.

The zombie pigman said, "It's just a coincidence. We don't all have names like that." He paused for a moment and then he asked, "I don't mean any offense, but did you just fart?"

Everyone in class except for Stan laughed at me. I hung my head in shame. I looked up and said, "Yes. It's a medical condition. I can't help it."

The zombie pigman shrugged. "I really don't care. As long as they don't smell too bad."

The class all laughed at me again.

"Well, Zane, they usually do," I said, not wanting him to be shocked by the stench should he ever be unlucky enough to smell it.

The zombie pigman nodded his head with understanding. "I see. Thank you for the warning. If you just stay at the back of the line, that will be appreciated."

"Yes," said the blaze. "Farts are dangerous around fire. They can cause explosions."

Again the class laughed at me. *Explosions, what did he mean by that?*

I was going to asked the blaze about it later, but mean old Josh Green beat me to it. "Bernie, what do you mean farts can cause explosions?"

The blaze looked at Josh and responded, "You didn't know? Fart gas is flammable."

I was shocked. I had no idea.

Josh turned and looked at me and sneered and said, "So you're telling me that Bart the Fart over there has a TNT factory inside his stomach?"

Everyone laughed at me. The teacher, stifling a laugh of her own, scolded the children. "Don't laugh at

Bart. You know it's a condition. He can't help it."

The other chaperone, Mrs. Coal, came over to me and said, "Sorry kid. But you had better keep your distance from blazes, torches, and lava while we are down there. You don't want to cause ... hurrr ... an incident."

I nodded my head in understanding. "Sure thing. I'll be careful."

The topic of my now explosive gas exhausted, the zombie pigman clapped his hands together and said, "Okay. How about that tour?"

Chapter 7

The tour of the Nether was actually really fascinating. Unfortunately, sometimes I had trouble seeing or hearing because I was stuck in the back of the class in order to avoid grossing everyone out with my farts, but I still had a good time.

The first place we were taken was to a cavern in which several dozen magma cubes resided. They were jumping up and down and acting silly and apparently having a good time.

When we entered the chamber, Bernie the blaze said in a loud voice, "Cubes! Calm down. We have visitors."

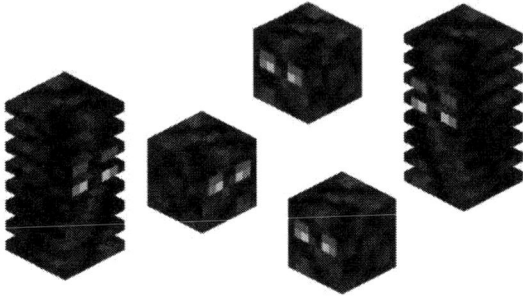

The cubes seemed more like villager toddlers because they didn't calm down and didn't seem to hear Bernie. Bernie had to yell at them again before they finally started to calm down. It took about two minutes before they were completely silent.

And of course, right when everything was perfectly quiet and no one was saying anything, I ripped a gigantic fart.

FRRRRAAAAA –
PUTTTOOOOOOOMMMMMMM –
SHAKA-LAKA!

The magma cubes all said, "Eeew." And then started laughing.

The thing about farts is if no one laughs, then everyone's disgusted, but if someone starts laughing, then everyone else thinks it's funny, even if it smells. So, because the magma cubes laughed, it deflected everyone's anger away from me and my massive echoing blast. However, it took the cubes another couple minutes to calm down from that distraction.

When it was quiet again, Bernie looked at me with his fiery eyes and asked, "Do you need to fart again?"

This drew some chuckles and a few titters from the magma cubes and my classmates, but no one laughed. I shook my head "no" and Bernie continued.

"Okay, children. These are magma cubes. They like to bounce around and have a good time. A lot of people from the Overworld consider them to be the Nether equivalent of slimes."

One of the magma cubes said, "We are not like slimes. We're not slimy."

Another magma cube chirped, "Yeah, slimes are green and disgusting. We're all dark-colored and awesome."

These magma cubes reminded me of five-year-old villagers, always trying to be more cool than anyone around them.

"But," said the zombie pigman, "they will attack players. Since you all are villagers, you should not worry about being attacked."

"Yeah, we love attacking players," said one of the cubes.

Cynthia Brown raised her hand. Bernie the blaze called on her and she asked, "So, if you guys attack players, how do you do that? Do you have weapons?"

The magma cubes laughed. One of them said, "Of course not. We *are* the weapons. We just jump on top of the players and squish them."

"Ouch. That sounds painful," said Cynthia.

I farted again, but it was barely a whisper. *Frizzeep.* I was standing at the back of the class, so the only person who heard me was Stanley. But he was wearing his anti-stink mask so he didn't mind.

Zane the pigman looked at everyone and said, "Any more questions?"

There were none and so we moved on.

The next place we came to was a very large chamber filled with several ghasts floating and meowing.

"Okay, kids. Now we come to a chamber filled with ghasts. They've all agreed to shoot a couple fireballs and then answer your questions," said Bernie.

We all watched in awe as two of the ghasts each shot a fireball across the chamber. It exploded with great force against the far wall of the chamber, shaking the very stones upon which we stood. The vibration shook loose a quiet but very stinky fart. *Phish.* It spread into the nearby area and several students expressed their disgust as they moved further away from me and Stan. By now, we were separated from the rest of our class by about five or six blocks of distance.

I looked over at Stan and said, "I wish I didn't fart so much. But all this excitement of the Nether is making me really gassy."

Stan shrugged. "You can't help it. It's no big deal."

But it was a big deal. I felt sad. I wondered what would happen when I grew up and Stan wanted to go to do something else or got married or moved to another village. Who would be my friend then?

Zane looked at all of us and said, "Any questions for the ghasts?"

Josh the bully raised his hand. When Zane called on him he said, "Hey ghasts. What makes you float? Are you filled with fart gas?"

All the kids in my class laughed. I even saw Mrs. Turtle and Mrs. Coal stifling a laugh. *I hate that guy*, I thought.

The ghasts looked at Josh with their humorless faces and said, "We are born with the ability to float. We do not contain fart gas."

"Yes," said another ghast. "And, if you stay down here long enough, maybe you'll float too."

The remaining ghasts in the chamber began to chant, "You'll float too. You'll float too."

For some reason, that last little bit made me feel uneasy. What did the ghast mean that he would "float too" if he stayed down here long enough? It made no sense. I looked over at our teacher and even she looked a little uneasy.

Zane looked at Bernie and winked at him and then turned back to us and said, "Okay kids, we've been on the tour for about an hour. Why don't you all sit down and have a snack."

"That sounds like a great idea, Mr. Porkchop," said our teacher. "Okay children, sit down and eat. The tour will resume soon."

Stanley and I sat down in a corner, keeping our distance from the rest of the crowd. I usually farted a lot when I ate, so I didn't want to cause any problems. I reached into my inventory and removed the chest of food my mom had given me earlier that day. Stanley had some food too. He had brought some watermelon, apples, and roasted chicken while my mom had packed me some mushroom stew and some dried kelp, as usual.

Stanley was nice enough to share some of his food with me. It was rare that I got to eat watermelons or roasted chicken, so it was quite a delight. Stanley rarely ate kelp or mushroom stew so he actually liked what I had.

Just as we were finishing up our snack, twenty-five zombie pigmen suddenly appeared as if from nowhere. They quickly surrounded the group and drew their golden swords.

Our teacher stood up and clasped her hand against her robe nervously. "What is the meaning of this?!?"

Zane looked at her with hate in his eyes and said, "You're being kidnapped. Don't resist."

My teacher began to sweat. Mrs. Coal also began to sweat and said, "Do what they say children. I'm sure this will all be over soon enough."

Bernie the blaze laughed and said, "The only way any of you are getting out of here is if your people give in to our demands."

"Demands?" asked Mrs. Turtle. "What demands?"

"We Nether mobs are sick of living here underneath the Overworld. We want a location in the Overworld where we can wander freely without being attacked by rampaging players.

We are going to demand the mayor of your village turn over the entire village to us or all of you will perish."

I looked at Stanley. He looked at me. We couldn't let this happen. It was time for action.

We were so far away from the rest of the group that the zombie pigmen had captured them without really paying attention us. In fact, I wasn't sure they even realized where we were. I looked to my left and saw a small crevice which appeared to open into a passageway. I moved my eyes back and forth toward the passageway until Stanley understood what I had planned. He nodded his head in agreement.

Without warning I ran as quickly as I could toward the passageway. Stanley followed me. As I ran, I pulled a torch from my inventory and ignited it so we could see where we were going.

At that moment Bernie noticed us and said to the zombie pigmen, "You idiots. Catch those two." Two zombie pigmen came after us. Because their legs were a lot longer than ours, they caught up with us pretty quickly. One reached a hand out and grabbed Stanley by the robe.

"Help, Bart!" yelled Stanley.

The next thing I did, I did without thinking. I tossed the torch so that it landed next to the zombie pigman's head. Then, I let out a massive fart – *SHABA DABA DOOO FRAAAAP!* – which bridged the gap between me and the zombie pigman in less than one second and created huge fireball, burning the zombie pigman.

The fireball inflicted enough damage that he screamed in pain before letting go of Stanley. I reached over near the angry zombie pigman and retrieved my torch. Stanley, now free, followed me into the darkness, the only light coming from the torch I gripped tightly in my right hand.

Chapter 8

After Stan escaped from the grasp of the zombie pigman, we ran for our lives. I'm not sure how much time passed, but I farted about a dozen times, so it must've been more than a minute.

When we finally felt we were out of harm's way, we stopped to regain our breath. I felt bad for Stan since he had been running behind me, breathing in my farts directly, his fart filtering mask had been lost during the escape. Fortunately, I still had on my double layer of wool and coal underwear, so some of the stench was reduced.

Stan was gulping massive breaths of air through his mouth, pinching his nostrils shut so he wouldn't have to smell what he was actually breathing. After he finally regained his breath, he said, "I don't believe it. Our entire class, our teacher, and the vice principal captured!"

I shivered with fear. "I know, it was shocking. How are we ever going to get back to the Overworld?"

"Well, we can find a Nether portal, and then all we have to do is jump in," said Stan.

"Great. Let's find one and get out of here," I said.

But then, as a sorrowful, silent fart slipped out, I realized that we couldn't leave our classmates behind. Sure, Josh the bully, Cynthia, and Jane were always mean to me, but the rest of the kids were cool, even though they all laughed at my farts. We couldn't just let them be held captive by the zombie pigmen who, if their demands were not met, would likely do something terrible and turn them all into puffs of smoke to respawn elsewhere.

"Actually, we need to rescue everybody, don't you think?" I said forcefully, a fart emphasizing my point. *Flabba-dabba-skree.*

Stan stood there silently, still breathing through his mouth and holding his nostrils shut. He was quiet for about ten seconds before he said, "Yes, I suppose we do. But how are we going to do that? We're just two ten-year-old villagers?"

I smiled mischievously. "Oh, that's true, but one of those ten-year-old villagers has a TNT factory in his stomach." I farted loudly as proof of concept. *SLAPPA-RAPPA-FLURP!*

Stan kept his hand on his nose, pinching it shut but said, "What do you mean?"

"We just need to figure out some way to capture all my gas in a container. Then all we have to do is ignite it somehow to cause an explosion. If we can do it in the right location, I'm sure we can knock the zombie pigmen down and free everybody."

Stan removed his fingers from his nose and said, "I don't know if it'll work, but I guess it's worth a try."

I nodded my head confidently. "How about this? We try to free them once and if we can't, we get to the nearest Nether portal and alert the authorities."

Stan stuck out his hand and shook mine. "Deal."

Chapter 9

We snuck back through the passageway where we had run away until we heard some zombie pigmen searching for us. At that point we veered off into a side passage, hoping it would eventually connect with the chamber where our classmates had been captured.

Fortunately, it did. And, even more fortunately, the connection was higher up in the chamber, meaning we were now perched on a ledge near the top of the chamber. This gave us a good view of everything that was happening.

Our classmates and the two adults with them had been herded into a small circle. A dozen zombie pigmen stood guard, preventing them from moving. Bernie the blaze and Zane Porkchop stood, looking slightly worried. Zombie pigmen ran into the chamber and reported to them and then ran away again.

I whispered to Stan, "They must be telling them that they have been unable to locate us."

Stan smiled. "Yes. And I'm sure they're very worried."

"Why?"

Stan scratched his cheek and said, "This is like some of those adventure books I read. If you're going to take hostages, you can't let any of them get hurt or get lost. If you do, the people you are negotiating with will think you're lying and not trust you. If they can't find us, they won't be able to make a deal."

I smiled. "Then maybe we should just stay hidden. If they can't find us after a while, they'll just let everyone go."

Stan shook his head. "Actually, they will probably just kill everybody and turn them into puffs of smoke. That way, they can make a point of how serious they were, the next time they manage to grab some hostages."

I sat there shaking my head, a silent but deadly fart leaking out. I found it difficult to believe there were mobs in the world that would treat young villagers like this. It made me sad. It also made me never want to visit the Nether ever again. I foresaw a life of trading with players for emeralds and books and compasses and whatever else I could manage to trade for.

"So, anyway, how are we going to capture your fart gas to make this bomb?"

I looked around for some sort of container in which to capture gas. I figured if we could contain enough of it, we could ignite it with a torch and that would be that.

"I can't think of anything that would work except my portable study area."

Stan looked at me in surprise. "You brought that with you?"

I nodded. "All the prior field trips we've been on they wanted me to bring it in case my farts smelled too nasty for everyone to handle. I have it in my inventory. Maybe we could set it up and then we could block the exhaust pipe and fill it full of gas."

Stan nodded his head and smiled. "I think it's a brilliant idea. Let's set up out of their line of sight."

The two of us walked back from the edge where we had been observing the scene, and I removed some glass blocks from my inventory. We first built a foundation made of wooden planks and then put the glass blocks on top of it. Where normally there would have been an exhaust pipe, I used a solid block instead.

"This looks great," said Stan. "Once you fill it full of gas, we can push it over the edge and then ignite it as it falls. It'll probably cause a huge explosion."

"Sounds good. I'm going in." I opened the door to the portable study area and sat down. I pulled out my kelp and mushroom stew from the food chest and started eating as fast as I could. I could feel the gas forming instantly in my stomach. I started farting so much that I thought I might deflate. Soon, this portable chamber was so full of gas I thought I myself might vomit. It was, to put it truthfully, disgusting.

After about fifteen minutes of this, I began to feel lightheaded, as though all the breathable air inside the chamber had been displaced by fart gas. I looked at Stan and held up my finger indicating I would be coming out in one second and for him to get ready to shut the door behind me. Stan gave me a thumbs up and stood at the ready.

I walked over the door and opened it quickly and stepped outside. Stan pulled the door closed behind me, trapping the gas inside.

I took some deep cleansing breaths and said, "So how do we make this thing blow up?"

"I think we need to attach a bunch of torches to the outside of it. We can light the torches and then when we push it over the edge, the glass will shatter and the torches will ignite the fart gas as it releases. That should cause enough of a distraction and an explosion that we can get everyone to come with us to the Nether portal."

I nodded my head. "Do you want to go down and lead them away or do you want to push the bomb over the edge?"

"How about I lead them away? I think that will actually be more dangerous than what you're doing. Once the bomb goes off, I'm sure it will dispose of some of the zombie pigmen and the rest will chase after us. You can bring up the rear and if any zombie pigmen pursue you, you can just fart on them."

I stifled a laugh. I guess I *could* just fart on them.

I gave Stan a couple of minutes to work his way down to the lower chamber. When enough time had passed, I ignited all the torches attached to the outside of the glass box and pushed the gas-filled cube over the edge.

It fell straight down, landing on top of three zombie pigmen, killing them instantly. The glass then shattered as it hit the ground and when the fart gas was released and connected with the torches, a massive explosion erupted, equivalent to several TNT blocks. The explosion killed about half of the zombie pigmen in the room and knocked most of the others to the ground. Only Zane and Bernie managed to stay vertical.

Once the blast wave from the fart bomb subsided, I heard Stan yell, "This way! Follow me to the portal!"

The startled members of my class and the two adults realized this was a rescue attempt and got up and ran as fast as they could after Stan. Zane and Bernie followed in pursuit with a couple of zombie pigmen straggling behind. After they left the room I ran down as fast as I could to follow them to the portal.

I could hear Zane and Bernie yelling, "No! We have to stop them!"

But they were too late. The entire class and the two adults had made it into the Nether portal, and all Zane and Bernie could do was stand there, screaming with rage.

And that's the exact moment I ran into the portal room.

Chapter 10

I stood there in shock as Bernie and Zane turned around, hatred, anger, and vengeance clearly visible in their eyes. Bernie pointed to the two zombie pigmen and then at me. "Get him!"

The two zombie pigmen lunged at me but I ducked away, blasting a huge fart right in their faces as they fell to the ground. *FRAA-zababidiblooop.* They coughed uncontrollably, and one of them even barfed.

"I don't believe this!" said Zane. "A kid farts on you and you're incapacitated?"

The zombie pigmen were too busy rolling on the ground in pain and agony to respond.

Zane shook his head in disgust. "When you want something done right, you have to do it yourself!"

Bernie and Zane began to approach me. Bernie from one direction and Zane from another. I could tell they were going to try to cut off my escape route either back into the Nether or forward into the Nether portal. But I had another idea.

As the Zane came closer, I suddenly ran as fast I could *directly at*

Zane. Zane laughed at my apparent stupidity, easily grabbing me and picking me up. I flailed my arms as hard as I could and he squeezed them down to stop me from moving.

Bernie the blaze approached from behind. He too was laughing at me. "What a stupid child."

But they had both miscalculated. As Zane squeezed me to keep me from flailing my arms, he forced out a huge burst of fart gas – *GURGL-ZURRFRAPP* – which landed directly on Bernie's burning body. It caused a minor explosion, severely damaging Bernie's health bar and knocking him unconscious to the ground.

Zane, in his surprise, loosened his grip slightly. I kicked him in the stomach. I heard him say, "Oof," as he dropped me.

I ran toward the Nether portal. Just as I was about to jump in I felt an undead hand grab my ankle. I looked back. It was Zane. His face was so close that it seemed huge.

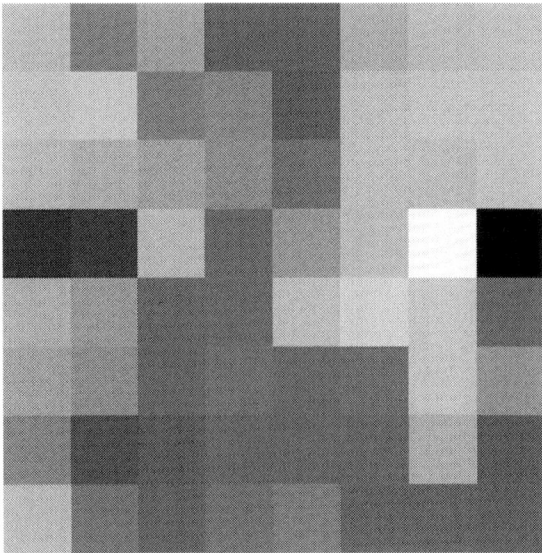

He said with his half zombie half pig mouth, "You are not going to get away."

I thought at that moment, he might be right. But then, I remembered that when I'm scared I fart even more than when I'm excited. A staccato burst of at least a dozen farts quickly came out – *trap zap nnnlo fraanit zagga meeseeks zoomba yabbadabba schlumburd frhhhooot zingt aamingto* – and blasted Zane right in the face. It was too much, even for an undead creature used to breathing the putrid smell of rotting flesh.

Zane coughed and let go of my leg, bringing his hands over his mouth and nose and gagging with disgust.

I stood up and ran toward the Nether portal never looking back. Just looking forward. And jumping through.

Chapter 11

When I came out the other side of the Nether portal, everyone was there waiting for me. Stan ran up to me and gave me a hug. I farted in response but I hugged him back. *Zooptodillit.*

I heard Mrs. Turtle say, "All praise be to Notch! Bart is alive!"

Josh the bully along with Cynthia and Jane walked up to me and said, "Stan told us about how you guys made that bomb. That was pretty cool!"

"It sure was. It's a good thing you have uncontrollable gas," said Jane.

Cynthia smiled at me. "I'm sorry I was so mean to you all these years. Who knew that your terrible defect would actually turn out to be the greatest weapon a ten-year-old villager has ever possessed."

Although I was happy I had saved my classmates and was glad to be away from the Nether myself, this ridiculous fake drama and fake praise was too much for me. I couldn't take it.

Still, I wanted to be polite. "Yeah, thanks guys. I think I just want to go home now."

Principal Blockhead ran over to make sure we were okay. He told us he had alerted the village police, who would send a force into the Nether to deal with these renegades Zane and Bernie. "If the police can't catch them, we will put a bounty on their heads. Every player across the Overworld will come try to collect it. Zane and Bernie won't stand a chance."

"That's cool," I said, as I farted. *Tooti-loop-di-doop.* "I'm going home now."

Chapter 12

When I got home I told my parents what happened. They were both in shock. My mom started crying, saying things about how she almost lost me and she will never let me go anywhere again. I didn't believe her. That's just typical mom stuff.

What did surprise me though was that I saw a few tears fall from my dad's eyes. I think they were a mixture of pride and sadness. He said, "Bart, I'm so glad you're alive. And, you did a great thing by saving your classmates when you could have, and probably should have, just run."

I smiled. "Thanks, Dad. Maybe now they'll want to talk to me instead of making fun of me because I fart."

My dad smiled, but looked unconvinced. "Maybe. Let's hope so."

*　*　*

I got up the next day and ate breakfast as usual and met Stan at the door. He was wearing a new fart-filter mask as we talked about our near-death experience. Other than that, it was a day like any other.

When I walked into the classroom though, I saw things were different. My glass study cell was gone. In its place was a desk with a new exhaust window cut in the wall. And, all the kids were wearing fart-filter masks, just like Stan's!!!

I looked over at Stan and asked, "Did you make these for everybody?" I could feel a tear of joy forming in my eye. But to my surprise Stan shook his head.

"Well, if you didn't make them, then ... hurrr ... who did?"

The voice that answered my query surprised me. "I did," said Josh.

"But I thought you did not know how to craft anything?"

Josh looked a little embarrassed and said, "Actually, until yesterday I really couldn't. But knowing you risked your life for all of us, I realized what a horrible person I've been all these years. And I asked my parents to help me learn how to craft fart-filter masks out of wool and coal. I stayed up past midnight making all these for everyone in class so you would not have to sit in that stupid glass box anymore. And, we might even be able stand being around you during recess."

On the inside, I felt like crying with joy. But on the outside, I didn't want to give Josh the bully the satisfaction. After all those years of mistreatment, I didn't want him to know how much his gesture meant to me. Maybe I was being petty not telling him the truth, but I just wasn't ready to be nice to someone who had been mean to me so much. Still, I said, "Thanks, Josh. Maybe we can play a game at recess. We could even be on the same team."

I could tell Josh was smiling behind his mask. "Sure thing, Bart."

That was the first time he said my name without making a fart reference. "Thanks."

"Yeah, sure. I think maybe you should have a new nickname. Something like the Gassy Bomber or the Zombie Pigman Roaster."

I shook my head. "How about we just go with Bart for now?"

The End

A Word from M.T. Lott

I hope you liked my second Minecraft-based fart story. I had fun writing it. Would you like to see me write more stories about farts set in the Minecraft universe? If you do, **tell me about it in your review** of the book on your favorite online bookstore or book review site.

Stay up to date on new releases by signing up for my email list at **mtlottbooks.com** or following me on Instagram @**mtlottbooks**.

And, if you like farts as much as I do, be sure to check out my other fart books, including:

Diary of a Farting Ghast

The Farting Animals Coloring Book

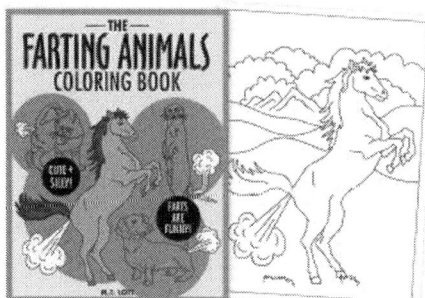

Farting Magical Creatures Coloring Book

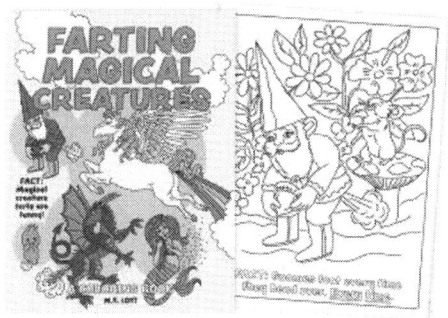

Annabelle the Reluctant Fart Fairy

Printed in Great Britain
by Amazon